Usborne

WRITE and DESIGN
YOUR OWN
MAGAZINES

Psst... there are pages at the back you can cut up to use in your own magazines.

Written by Sarah Hull

Illustrated by Ro Ledesma, James Daw, Joe List and Irena Freitas

Designed by Freya Harrison

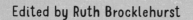

Edited by Ruth Brocklehurst   Series designer: Laura Wood

Contents

Starting out

Decide what your magazine is going to be about and start collecting ideas.

Get writing

What should I review?

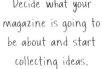

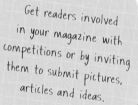

Get readers involved in your magazine with competitions or by inviting them to submit pictures, articles and ideas.

Making pictures

There are lots of ideas for ways to make your magazine pages look bold and fun.

Find out how to make all kinds of magazines, from fold-outs and pocket-sized booklets to cabinets filled with curiosities.

Putting it all together

USBORNE QUICKLINKS

For links to websites where you can read magazines for inspiration, get drawing tips, create comic strips, and download pictures and patterns, go to www.usborne.com/quicklinks and type in the keyword "Magazines." Please follow the internet safety guidelines at the Usborne Quicklinks website. Children should be supervised online.

Over to you...

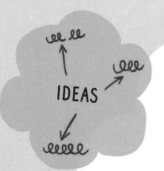

IDEAS

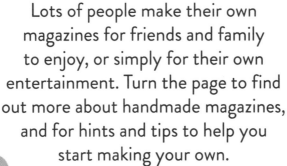

Starting out

Lots of people make their own magazines for friends and family to enjoy, or simply for their own entertainment. Turn the page to find out more about handmade magazines, and for hints and tips to help you start making your own.

?

What are handmade magazines?

Handmade magazines or "zines" are really fun to make, read and collect. Filled with pictures, stories and articles, they come in all shapes and sizes, and can cover all kinds of themes. Browse these pages to see for yourself.

MY PET MONSTER

UP, UP AND AWAY

My stamp collection

VOTES FOR UNDER 18S

Personal interests

EMOTICONS

Lots of zines are inspired by personal passions, or by ordinary, everyday life.

puNk ZINE

Fruit & veggies

DAILY DOODLES

Hobbies

TUNE TITANS

Basketball hotshots

my top 5 magic tricks

Meeting my hero

Real-life events

THE FAMILY NEWS

They are often made by just one person, but they can be a team effort.

A day in the life

Strange but True

Plant life

Cats! Cats!

Comics

HI!

Zines are great for showcasing your writing or drawings – or both.

the TALL zine

Something you know lots about...

Harry Potter fanzine

CRACKING THE ENGIMA CODE

INSTRUCTION MANUAL FOR PARENTS

Some zines have just pictures and no words.

Fanzines are magazines about books, music or anything created by fans for other fans. FAN + magaZINE = FANZINE.

MINI ZINE

...or would like to know more about

Napkin folding

Birds

modern art

Something you've never really thought about before

13 THINGS THAT GO BUMP IN THE NIGHT

Find out different ways of making zines of all shapes and sizes on pages 54-59.

What if... I was the size of my hand?

Turn the page to start making your own...

What's it all about?

If you pick a theme for your magazine, it'll be a good starting point for your articles, pictures and stories. Your theme can be loose or specific. It can be a book, song or movie, inspired by history or even by asking a "what if..." question.

STUFF TO ENTERTAIN YOU OVER BREAKFAST

What if dogs were in charge and kept humans as pets?

SPOOKY STORIES

What if I were President?

Things written and drawn by me and my brother

The Wizard of Oz

Fashion

How to save the planet

What if I were the strongest person in the world? (Psst... see page 39.)

News from where I live

The Titanic

Travel dreams

BADGERS

My life

Write some of your own theme ideas here.

Choosing a title

Once you've chosen a theme, it's time to think about titles. A good title will grab the attention of your readers and make them want to take a closer look. So how do you come up with the perfect title?

Title tips

- Keep it relevant – link it to the theme.

- Think ahead. If you're planning on making more than one issue of your magazine, choose a title that will work for all of them – even if they have different themes.

- If your magazine is inspired by a book or movie, you could use a quotation as the title.

- Make it enticing. Try something short, catchy and easy to remember, or go for a long and intriguing title that will get readers interested.

You could add a subtitle to let readers know the theme of each issue.

CURIOUS
orange
Issue 2

CURIOUS
boredom

CURIOUS
jellyfish
Issue 1

The forgotten adventures of Alf, the computer that thought it was *a human*

Title ideas

BOUNCE - for basketball fanatics

UP, UP AND AWAY - about travel dreams

SPOOKY - full of spooky stories

TAKE YOUR TIME

If you think of a few good titles and can't choose between them, you might want to wait until you've gathered more ideas before making a final decision.

Gathering ideas

The next step is to start gathering ideas to do with your theme.
Think about the mix of writing and pictures you want to include, too.

You could collect ideas
in a list:

Gardens

- Tips for growing
vegetables (could illustrate
with potato prints)

- Garden pest picture quiz

- Review of *The Secret
Garden* by Frances
Hodgson Burnett

- All about bees and your
garden – amazing facts

- Recipes?

- Seed diary – sketches?

Some people like to arrange their ideas in a mind map.
To make one of these, write your theme or title in the
middle and collect a web of ideas around it.

Interview friends to
find out what they
do to look after the
planet – remember to
ask them for a photo.

Illustrate with
doodles of fish
and plastic?

Facts about plastic
in the oceans and its
impact on sea life

My diary as
a volunteer

HOW TO SAVE THE PLANET

Every minute,
a truckload of plastic
is dumped in the ocean.

Look up exactly
how much...

Ingenious ways to
consume less energy
and reduce waste

Comic – the characters could
be based on things you might
find in a recycling bin.

Recycle me!
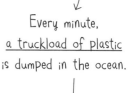

Make a sausage dog from old
socks to block gaps under doors.

Unplug
electronic devices
once they're
fully charged.

You can jot your ideas here.

TIP

Collect old newspapers and magazines for inspiration or to cut up and use in your mag.

You might find it helpful to decide what size and shape you want your magazine to be now, so you know how much space you have to fill. Turn to pages 54–59 for ideas.

A booklet is a smart choice for your first magazine. It'll be easy to put together, especially if you make sure all your articles and pictures fit on standard sheets of paper folded in half.

Get writing

Now it's time to start writing amusing articles, gripping stories, heartfelt opinion pieces and razor-sharp book reviews to fill your magazine. Grab your reporter's notebook so you can scribble down notes and ideas.

ARTICLES!

Haha!

Phenomenal!

Research

There are lots of different types of articles you can write for your magazines, from reports to opinion pieces. But before you start writing, you may want to research the subject a little more.

Find out more

- Go to your local library and read up on the subject.

- Watch the news and documentaries on TV.

- Visit relevant locations.

- Interview people – there are tips on page 22.

Library card

Return ticket

Keep a note of your sources: the books, articles and websites where your information comes from. You might need to check them later.

You should list your sources at the end of an article.

Personal accounts in letters can be sources too, but ask the author before you use them.

If you're stuck for ideas, the Usborne Quicklinks website has links to a selection of inspiring websites with helpful research and writing tips. Turn to the contents page for more information.

TIP

It's easier to make changes as you go if you're working on a computer. You can always write out an article by hand once it's finished.

Reports

If you want to tell people about a particular topic or event, you could write a report. Reports state the facts clearly and concisely.

- Only include information that's relevant.

- Avoid "I" or "you" where possible.

- Back up statements with facts, figures and expert opinions.

- Explain who people are when you first mention them.

Weird weather

Snow was piled high on Ambrose Lane this week, in what the Weather Office confirms is the coldest April since records began. Children celebrated the unseasonal snow by building snowmen.

Cecily Cumulus, the Lane's oldest resident, said, "I've lived here for almost 70 years and I've never seen anything like this before!" She believes climate change is responsible for this weird weather.

> Has anything unusual happened that you could report on?

Listicles

Articles written like lists are called listicles. They can be an entertaining way of bringing together lots of different ideas and thoughts.

11 things parents do to embarrass their children

1. Sing loudly in public. This is especially embarrassing if they can't sing in tune.

2. Display baby photos prominently for visitors to see.

7 ways to work more effectively

1. Make a to-do list to break down everything you need to do into achievable tasks.

2. Go for a run.

14 books I loved reading

1. The Lord of the Rings

2. Animal Farm

3. The Railway Children

4. Goodnight Mister Tom

Explaining why you've chosen each point will make your list more persuasive.

Opinion pieces

An opinion piece is a persuasive article with a personal touch – perfect for a topic you feel passionate about, whether that's endangered species, rights for young people or school meals.

Explain what you think and why. Don't get too caught up in facts and figures.

Write from your point of view.

The Usual Park may not look like anything special, but I absolutely love it. It's an oasis of calm in the busy city, perfect for when you need a breath of fresh air. Sadly, there are plans to build a new supermarket on the grounds of the park.

Address your readers directly.

If the Usual Park matters to you even half as much as it does to me, please attend the meeting at the town hall on Thursday at 6pm to discuss the plans.

You could finish your piece with a call to action.

Some opinion pieces are designed to amuse. In these, you can exaggerate your feelings for comic effect.

R.I.P. Snizzles

From this day forth, I renounce all chocolate. I'm doing this in memory of Snizzles, the tastiest, most exquisite of chocolate bars, which you can't buy anywhere anymore.

Headlines

Here are some tips for giving your articles headlines that will grab readers' attention and make them want to read on.

Headlines should be intriguing and tell you what an article is about.

Try using a question as a headline.

Keep headlines short, and don't give away the whole story.

Try wordplay, such as rhymes or repeating the same letter sound.

THE TRUTH ABOUT LYING

When was the last time you lied? More likely than not, you did it to be kind...

SKIN CRAWLING?

No? Wait till you've read this... Scientists estimate that there are around a trillion microbes living on your skin right now.

~~A CAT BURGLAR GOT STUCK IN A CATFLAP WHILE ESCAPING FROM THE SCENE OF A CRIME.~~

CRIMINAL CAUGHT IN CATFLAP

Borrowed words

If you don't feel like writing, you could create a short article using borrowed words.

Thunderbolts

artisanal

Extreme sports

Frequently

Use twice a week for silky soft hair.

The first tiger I met

Rising prices

grumbling

This is perfect for when you have writer's block.

Simply cut out words and phrases from old newspapers and magazines. Then arrange them to make nonsense news bulletins or tall tales.

From July

The President won't be taking

unusually sweaty

toads

SERIOUSLY!

To use words from a book, photocopy the page, then cut up the copy.

Telling stories

Everyone loves a good story. When you write stories for your magazines, make sure you add these three crucial ingredients...

Convincing characters

Try to make the people you are writing about believable. Ideally, readers should want to spend time with them as well.

Make sure there are plausible reasons why characters behave the way they do, and don't make them too perfect. Even a hero should have fears, doubts and flaws.

> I'm going to destroy Jay's writing career because I am jealous. NO ONE APPRECIATES *MY* POETRY!

A compelling plot

In the most satisfying stories, each event happens for a reason and builds on what's happened before.

A message in a bottle. → So the hero sets sail to rescue Meg. → Stormy weather blows the boat off course...

Please help! Meg

...and to a previously undiscovered island.

And then...

An unexpected turn of events, known as a twist, can stop a plot from becoming predictable. This could be a case of mistaken identity.

> I'm not out to get you – I'm your mother!

Can't think of a character to write about? Why not borrow one?

Stories based on existing ones are known as fan fiction.

A sense of time and place

Weaving in details about the world where a story is set can help make it more vivid.

The planet Zogton in a galaxy far, far away...

Different, yet strangely familiar

Not as safe and luxurious as it first appears

Titanic

Plotting and planning

Jotting down a plan before you start writing will help you figure out if the plot makes sense and the pace of events feels right.

It might help to think of a story as a journey.

Uh oh...

2. The build-up

What do the main characters want, and what obstacles are stopping them from achieving their goal? Develop the problem and build it up.

1. THE START

Main character or characters

Who are we? Where are we? And what are we doing?

Possible obstacles:
- A villain
- A crisis of confidence
- A force of nature

It's no good – I'm not brave enough...

3. The dramatic climax

This is the make-or-break moment when everything could go horribly wrong. Does it?

Introduce new characters. Are they helpful? Do they cause problems?

Ahhh!

Which way now?

4. The descent

Your characters have survived the worst of it. Now it's time to clear up any other problems.

Nearly there...

5. THE END

Did everyone make it? How has the journey changed things?

Ahhh...

Or you could crank up the suspense for one last drama.

Drama

Grr!

Microfiction

Tantalize your readers with microfiction – incredibly short tales that hint at a much larger story. Microfiction is usually no longer than 100 words, but it can be even shorter.

Author Ernest Hemingway is said to have written a story in just six words for a competition:

"For sale: baby shoes, never worn."

NIGHTMARE

Kay trotted downstairs for breakfast. He couldn't wait to tell his family about the strange dream he'd had where he'd been a cat.

But when he entered the kitchen, there was someone just like him already sitting at the table, and all he could say was, "meow!"

Try building a story around a creepy revelation or a joke.

There's no space in microfiction for introducing characters or setting the scene. You need to get straight to the action.

You could start with an intriguing line of dialogue.

"Wrong number," said my mother, hanging up on me.

Your turn...

You could cut down a longer story you've written.

Try retelling a familiar story, such as a fairy story, using 100 words, or even just ten.

To be continued...

Rather than including a *whole* story in your magazine, you could include a chapter and continue the story in the next issue.

Author Charles Dickens wrote *Great Expectations*, *Oliver Twist* and many other novels, chapter by chapter, for weekly or monthly literary magazines. Here are some of the techniques he used to keep readers hooked...

Emotional appeal

Dickens's stories appealed to readers' emotions, with laugh-out-loud comedy and tragedy designed to reduce them to tears.

Captivating characters

Dickens created memorable characters that stayed in readers' minds. They often have distinctive ways of speaking or striking appearances.

Miss Havisham from *Great Expectations*

"She was dressed in rich materials – satins, and lace, and silks – all of white. Her shoes were white. And she had a long white veil dependent from her hair, and she had bridal flowers in her hair, but her hair was white..."

Cliffhanger

Ending a chapter with a cliffhanger – a dramatic or uncertain situation – left readers desperate to find out what happened next.

Wait and see

Dickens didn't finish these stories before the first chapters were published. Sometimes he waited for readers to react before deciding how to continue.

Make 'em laugh, make 'em cry, make 'em wait!

Charles Dickens

INK

Interviews

If you want to write about a person, you could interview them and use their own words. You could ask friends or family members if you can talk to them – or make up an interview with a fictional character, such as Sleeping Beauty or a character from a cartoon.

Do you have any advice on how to conduct a good interview?

Have a list of questions you want to ask. Six or so should be enough. But don't stick rigidly to your list. Follow up on interesting things your interviewee says.

Make your interviewee feel at ease – you'll get better answers.

Interviews don't have to be conducted in person – you can quiz someone on the phone, or send questions in an email or by mail.

Try to ask open-ended questions, such as "What do you think about fishing?" rather than ones that might get a "yes" or "no" answer.

Jot down notes or record the interview on a phone so you can listen to it again.

Most of your interviews will be with friends or family. If you do manage to set one up with someone else, take a grown-up with you for company.

Thank you all for your answers.

Writing it up

You don't have to include everything that was said when you write up an interview. Cut it down to just the most interesting and exciting parts.

The Big Sleep

A conversation with fairy tale star Sleeping Beauty

– A J Pineapple

I met Sleeping Beauty at a truly magical cafe. Fairy cakes fluttered around our heads as we spoke.

AJP: You must get asked this a lot – what was it like to sleep for a hundred years?

SB: ~~Um. Well..~~ It actually felt just like an ordinary night's sleep. That made waking up incredibly strange. I didn't feel like I'd been asleep long, yet everything was different ... Beyond the sleeping castle's walls, the world had changed completely. I'd missed world wars, women getting the vote, Harry Potter, the invention of computers, cell phones and so many other things.

Make it clear who's saying what.

Start by setting the scene and introducing your interviewee.

Cut out any pauses, hesitations and filler words.

If you cut part of the interview, insert a " ... " to show where text has been removed.

Write a couple of sentences at the end of the interview to sum it up. You could say whether your interviewee was as you'd expected, and if not, how he or she was different.

On the record?

Some things in an interview may be said unofficially – or "off the record" – with the understanding that you won't include them in your magazine.

Always show your interviewee the finished article before you print it. That way any mistakes can be corrected.

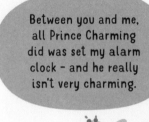

Between you and me, all Prince Charming did was set my alarm clock – and he really isn't very charming.

Reviews

Tell your readers about good things to do, read, see and visit – and help them avoid terrible experiences – by including reviews in your magazines. You can review anything, from books and movies, to recipes, museums or even your local swimming pool.

Start with a couple of sentences introducing what you're reviewing.

Justify your statements by explaining why you formed that opinion.

Aztec Living at the Museum of Old is the best exhibition I've ever seen. The displays include extraordinary objects and show what life was like in Mexico hundreds of years ago.

The broccoli was so overcooked it had fallen apart. My fork was useless – I had to spoon the gloop into my mouth.

When I pointed out the problem, the waiter said he thought I'd asked for the soup. The gloop was whisked away and replaced with a heap of broccoli stalks, cooked to perfection.

Bad reviews can be entertaining to read...

...but be fair – mention both the good and the bad to give a full picture.

End your review by summing up your opinion. Let your readers know whether they should read the book, see the movie, try the recipe... or give it a miss.

SPOILER ALERT

It's fine to hint at plot twists or say the ending of a book is fantastic, but avoid spoilers – descriptions that will ruin the surprise or lessen the suspense.

This action-packed story keeps you guessing right to the end. Read it now! Trust me, you won't be able to put it down.

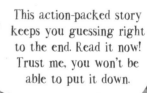

Rating systems, such as stars, give readers a quick overview of what you thought.

Underwhelming

A predictable plot and plodding performances made for a disappointing evening at the movies.

TIP

It's easier to write a review of something you have strong opinions about. Pick something you love or hate.

BEST CAKE EVER!

This recipe for chocolate cake will make you incredibly popular – if you choose to share the results, that is.

You could award cakes, hearts, flowers or smiley faces instead of stars.

If you're not sure what to review...

Riveting   Heartwarming

Breath-taking   Fascinating

REPULSIVE   Melts in the mouth

Have you ever read a book so good you couldn't put it down?

Where's the most extraordinary place you've been this year?

Picturesque   Bustling

What are the best and worst things you've eaten this week? Describe them.

Spellbinding

Poignant   Sickly sweet

Page-turning

STOMACH-TURNING   Crumbly   TWO-FACED

CRUEL

Is there a book, or place, that never fails to cheer you up?

What's the most toe-curlingly awful movie you've ever seen?

Can you think of any characters that really annoy you?

Dazzling   Surprising

Terrifying   Mind-numbingly dull   Whining

25

Calling all readers!

Make your readers feel appreciated by getting them involved in your mag. You could invite them to...

...vote for the greatest cookie of all time.

...send in comments to print on a letters page.

...take part in a caption contest.

One lucky entrant's name and caption will be printed in the next issue.

...send in jokes, comics, pictures or articles to include in your next mag.

Hahaha!

WOW!

Make sure you say when the deadline is and what you're going to do with the things people send you.

...suggest a theme for the next issue.

 Stationery

Musicals

The zombie apocalypse

...let you know which feature in your magazine they enjoyed most.

...draw a picture based on a prompt. You could print the best ones in the next issue.

Bad hair day

Dave Weasel, London

STAY SAFE

If you're asking people to send you things, ONLY give your postal or email address to people you know, and check with a grown-up first.

Advice columns

You could include an advice column in your magazine, where readers' tricky questions are answered.

I need your help!

My wonderful grandma knitted me a sweater for my birthday, but it's really scratchy and uncomfortable. What should I say to her?

Yours gratefully, Mr. Itchy

The questioner's identity is kept secret. Column writers usually invent a name that relates to the problem.

The golden rule of receiving presents is that every gift is worth a "thank you." Make sure you let your grandma know how grateful you are that she took the time to make you a sweater.

You also need to decide whether to be honest. If you want to avoid hurting her feelings, you could try wearing it when you know you're going to see her, maybe with a T-shirt under it. However, if she's an avid knitter, it might be wise to tell her a kind version of the truth, for instance, "It's a teeny bit itchy."

Wishing you luck!

Agony Aunt Agnes

Try to avoid telling people what to do. Instead, make suggestions:

"Have you considered...?"

"You might want to..."

"...works for me."

Ask Agnes!

You could create a friendly character to be the name and face of your advice column.

Ye olde problems

The first known advice column appeared in 1691, in a London magazine called **The Athenian Mercury**. The editor formed a "society of experts" to answer questions. Here are some of them:

Why is thunder more terrible in the night time?

Dancing, is it lawful?

How can a man know when he dreams or when he is really awake?

Working with others

You may want to make your magazine on your own, but if not, getting others involved will introduce lots of new ideas and different voices.

- Do you want an article, advice column, comic or interview? Should it be on a particular topic? Make sure you let people know. It would be a shame for someone to spend hours working on something you won't be able to use.

- Tell them how long a piece of writing you'd like – or how much space is available.

- Will you give them anything in return?

Please will you write a terrifying tale of 500–1,000 words for my magazine SPOOKY? Your story can be about anything, as long as it's creepy and unsettling.

I'll give you a free copy of SPOOKY in return for your story.

Let them know if you'd like them to send in pictures as well as words.

MAKE FRIENDS NOT ENEMIES!

If you're going to include other people's work, make sure you have permission to do so, and that you include their names with their pieces.

The abominable seagull
A tale of ice-cream theft and seaside sadness
by Tess Haldrick

The ghoul in the garage
by Ben Ahuja

Space fillers

Here are some ideas for ways you can fill any blank spaces or empty pages.

What's hot and what's not?

List the latest trends in hairstyles, smoothies, reading or whatever you like. Make sure you let your readers know what is "so last year," too...

HOT
Novelty bookmarks

Homemade magazines

Big pockets for carrying books

NOT
Reading while walking - that's just dangerous!

Quizzes

Put your readers to the test with puzzling questions, for example:

1 Where would you find the Sea of Tranquility?

a The Pacific

b The Moon

c The planet Mars

2 Where will you put the answers?

a On a page at the back of your magazine.

b In small writing, upside-down at the bottom of the page.

c In the next issue, so readers will want to read that, too.

Puzzles

Get readers to exercise their brains with puzzles and brainteasers.

You can make puzzles with pictures, too.

Can you find these puzzle words in the grid?

wordsearch

enigma

crossword

riddle

maze

number

```
c r o s e l d d r a e
r r o e n i g m a z n
o w o r d s e a r c h
c r o s b o r z n r s
e d m i s a b e r o o
n b s a g w r i d d l
r e g i e r o s b e b
a i n u m b e r b n s
s e d z a z e n d p e
a r l e l d d i r e s
```

Answers: 1 = b; 2 = up to you!

29

Editing

Make sure you edit any writing before it goes in your magazine. Editing isn't only about correcting errors, it's also an opportunity to cut out any waffling and check that everything is as clear as possible.

First, read through your writing to check it makes sense.

- Have you missed out any steps in your explanations or plot?

- Have you explained who everyone is?

> Who's *she*? The cat's mother?

> She picked up the kitten and gave him a lick.

Next, read it aloud. Over-used words, mistakes and weak points often stand out more when you hear them out loud.

> I like to use lots of fluffy-wuffy, waffly-baffly, unnecessary, non-essential, pointless adjectives that are surplus to requirement when I describe things.

> Not so many, please – all the words should serve a purpose.

If a word feels a bit flat, use a thesaurus to find another word with the same meaning that's more exciting or precise.

> When the monster spoke, her voice was **LOUD**.

EAR-SPLITTING
BOOMING
DEAFENING
THUNDERING
POWERFUL
RUMBLING ROARING STENTORIAN
BLARING DEEP RICH

THESAURUS

Finally, read your writing through slowly, checking the grammar and punctuation and looking out for spelling mistakes. You might find it helps to start with the final sentence and work back.

Usborne Quicklinks

Get help with grammar, punctuation and spelling via the Usborne Quicklinks website.

Spellcheckers can help check for misspellings on a computer, but they won't spot every error.

Common mistakes to watch out for

It's and its

If you can use **it is** or **it has** instead, then the correct word is **it's**.

Repeated and ~~and~~ missing words.

He ~~should of~~ should have used a dictionary.

Never **should of**

Rafi felt the ~~affect~~ effect of the love potion immediately.

Effect is the noun, **affect** is the verb.

She read neither book ~~or~~ nor comic.

Nor follows **neither**, **or** follows **either**.

Noah and Freya ~~likes~~ like pizza.

No **s** on the end of the verb when there's more than one person doing the action.

The flock of swans ~~look~~ looks threatening.

Not **look** because **flock** is the subject and there is only one flock.

THAT'S A GOOD IDEA...

A second pair of eyes can be really helpful. Is there someone you could ask to read through your writing to look out for mistakes?

If you're editing someone else's writing, make sure they are happy with any changes or corrections you make.

Making pictures

This section is crammed with ideas for ways you can make, take and draw pictures to bring your magazines to life. And fear not: you don't need to be an amazing artist to create great pictures.

CHEESE!

Using pictures

You can do all sorts of things with pictures in your magazines. For instance, you could illustrate an article or a poem, make a picture diary, show how to do something or create an advertisement.

You could make words and pictures fit around each other.

Illustrations don't have to have a hard border.

"BEWARE THE JABBERWOCK, MY SON! THE JAWS THAT BITE, THE CLAWS THAT CATCH!"

From Lewis Carroll's poem "Jabberwocky"

A day at the beach

We all had fun, except for Dad.

BEING TIDY

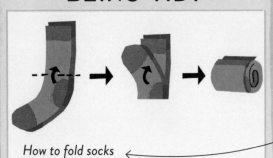

How to fold socks

You might want to add a *caption* to your image to make its meaning clearer...

Putting pictures in boxes with straight edges can help make a page look neat and tidy. Place the image on the page with the same amount of space on each side, then arrange text into a rectangular block above or below it.

...or to say what the title is and who created it.

Design for a Sandcastle by James Zuma, August 15

To make a big impact, you could run a picture right to the edge of the page.

Most home printers and photocopiers can't print right to the edge, so you'll need to trim the page after printing if you want to do this.

TIP

If you haven't already chosen a size and shape for your magazine, turn to pages 54-59 for ideas. Whatever you're illustrating, you'll need to measure how much room there is before you start.

Thinking ahead

You may only want to make one copy of your magazine, but if you do plan to make more, the way you print may affect how you choose to make your pictures.

Turn to page 63 to read about printing.

If you're planning on making copies with a photocopier, make sure details are dark and defined enough to print clearly. Black pen or paint may be clearer than a pencil sketch.

Another important decision is whether to print in black and white or color.

If you work in black and white, pictures are easier to print or photocopy. Plus, there's no need to worry about clashing - black and white go with *everything*.

Rainbow colors can be very eye-catching, but printing in color is usually more expensive. Results can be a little unpredictable, too - especially if an ink cartridge is running low.

Cut-and-paste pictures

Here are some ideas for making pictures by cutting out paper shapes and arranging them. This technique is known as collage, which is French for "gluing."

There are pages of decorated paper at the back of this book you can use.

Try painting or decorating paper to cut shapes from.

You could make a collage with shapes cut from patterned paper or scraps of rough paper.

Things don't have to make sense – let your imagination go wild.

Cut out pictures from old newspapers and glossy magazines to make into new pictures.

Start with the biggest shapes, then add smaller details.

You could take your own photos to cut out and use in a collage.

Old newspaper or sheet music can make interesting patterns in pictures.

Arrange the pieces first, then glue them down when you're satisfied with how it all looks.

Cut-and-paste characters

Collage is a great way of inventing extraordinary characters to use in comics or to illustrate articles and stories. These characters might even inspire new ideas.

TIP
Keep leftover snippings to make cut-and-paste doodles and to decorate pages.

You could draw on extra details.

LIFE ON MARS

BOOKWORM CHRONICLES

Sketches

Hearsay

I'm Librosaurus - a living, breathing library that always knows what magazine you should read next.

Experiment with different options for legs.

If your character appears more than once, instead of gluing the pieces down, photograph them in one position...

...then rearrange the pieces, adding any extra bits you need, and photograph them again.

AH...

...TCHOO!

Goooorgeous darling - hold that pose!

Taking photos

You don't need loads of fancy equipment to take great photos. Just try out these tips and tricks with whatever camera you have, then print out the photos and stick them in your magazine.

It's all about the lighting

The way scenes or people are lit can transform how they appear in a photo.

"Photograph" means drawing with light in Ancient Greek.

Use a flashlight to create striking lighting when you pose for a photo.

Strong lighting from one direction can make interesting shadows.

The "golden hour" occurs just after sunrise and just before sunset. At these times, the light is redder and softer. It's meant to be a very flattering light for portraits.

Lighting objects front and back can help soften heavy shadows.

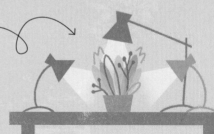

Harness technology...

If you're using a phone to take photos, you can apply filters to brighten or distort them.

Try using apps to decorate your pictures with "stickers" or effects.

...or don't

Alternatively, you could make your own filters.

Try taking photos through the lens of your sunglasses, through bubble wrap or a glass of water.

Make characters

Anything can become a character if you give it a face.

Arrange objects into different expressions to illustrate an article or story.

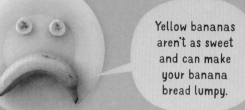

The best bananas for banana bread are overripe and brown.

Yellow bananas aren't as sweet and can make your banana bread lumpy.

Cliffhanger photo trick

Take a photo that makes it look as if someone is hanging off a cliff. Ask a friend to lie on the floor and pretend they're clinging to a wall with just one hand.

Crouch down and take a photo.

Rotate the photo on the screen so it's upside down, or print it out and turn it around.

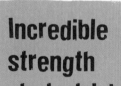

Incredible strength photo trick

Arrange a scene so someone looks as if they're lifting a person, building or object behind them.

In this photo the man is actually standing on a stool hidden behind the girl.

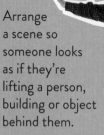

Comics

Comics, or comic strips, combine illustrated scenes and speech bubbles to tell stories, explain ideas or make jokes. People have been putting them in magazines for years and years, often to make a serious point in a comical way.

In comic strips, the scenes are normally arranged into boxes called panels. Panels can vary in size and shape to suit each scene. You usually read them from left to right.

Things can extend out of panels.

Sounds that aren't thoughts or speech are often written directly onto the panel.

Making comics

When you're making a comic, the first step is to decide what needs to go in each panel.

Write a brief description of what each scene will show and the captions, dialogue and sound effects you want to include.

PANEL 1

WHERE? At an art gallery. Show George looking at his stomach with a worried expression.

CAPTION: While visiting the art gallery, George started to feel very peculiar.

SOUND EFFECTS: Gurgling from George's belly.

Next, sketch out rough designs for the different panels.

Make sure your designs leave enough room for captions and speech bubbles.

Don't try to cram too much into each panel.

Waiting until the next page to reveal a plot twist is a great way to build suspense.

You can use comics to tackle a wide range of topics. Why not try making a comic...

...based on a story you like.

...imagining the humorous thoughts of an everyday object.

Can you believe he lost me again?!

...explaining how to do something, such as looking after a cactus, or making bread.

People have been making comics for hundreds of years. Just look at the Bayeux Tapestry...

...to bring a real historical event vividly to life.

...about an unlikely hero, or a criminal mastermind.

I've got all the cats on the run!

Characters for comics

All you need to make a character for your comic is a stick figure and some accessories.

Or if stick figures aren't your thing, start with a shape and give it arms, legs and a face.

With just a few lines and dots, you can give your characters faces that express a huge range of emotions.

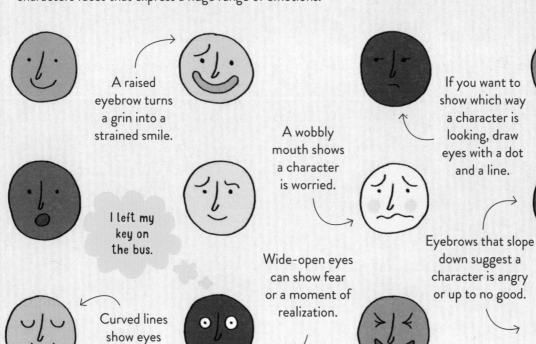

A raised eyebrow turns a grin into a strained smile.

I left my key on the bus.

A wobbly mouth shows a character is worried.

If you want to show which way a character is looking, draw eyes with a dot and a line.

Eyebrows that slope down suggest a character is angry or up to no good.

Curved lines show eyes are closed.

Wide-open eyes can show fear or a moment of realization.

Covers

First impressions matter, and that means covers have to be eye-catching. So... how do you make a cover that makes people want to pick up your magazine for a closer look?

The title should be big and stand out.

Include an issue number.

A bold picture will help grab attention.

Strong contrasts, like black and white or orange and blue, can be very striking.

Who's it by? You could add your real name, or a made-up pen name.

Add the price.

You could mention special features, such as exclusive interviews, competitions or other unusual content.

As you work on the cover, ask yourself:

Does it give an accurate impression of what my magazine is like inside?

Would I pick it up?

Look at magazines, book covers and advertisements for inspiration. What works and what doesn't?

Play with the lettering

Different styles of lettering (on computers these are called fonts) have different personalities. It's worth spending some time finding one that suits your magazine – especially for the title.

TIP!

Use the same font, or style of writing, for the title across different issues to help give your magazine a recognizable look.

Looks too serious → Woof!

Woof! ← Bouncy, but a little difficult to read

A touch shouty → WOOF!

WOOF! ← Fun and just a bit scruffy – like a dog!

Don't forget the back!

The back cover is another opportunity for getting readers interested in your magazine.

- Use a striking new picture, or continue a picture from the front cover onto the back cover.

- List the contents – or some of the highlights.

- You could write a blurb, a short description of your magazine to entice people to start reading.

- Quote nice things people have said about previous issues of your magazine.

"Essential reading for any dog lover."
– Dorothy & Toto

Which dog breed are you? Find out with our quiz.

Continued... The Adventures of Billy Bones, Welsh Terrier extraordinaire

Grooming tips for healthy fur

WOOF!
Issue 1
By Lucy Whippet

Free

FEATURES
An interview with Queen Elizabeth II's corgis

Top 10 dog breeds, as voted for by you!

And much more!

Printing covers by hand

If you want to make several copies of your magazine, but still give each copy a personal touch, you could print the covers by hand. You could use ready-made stamps, or make your own following these instructions.

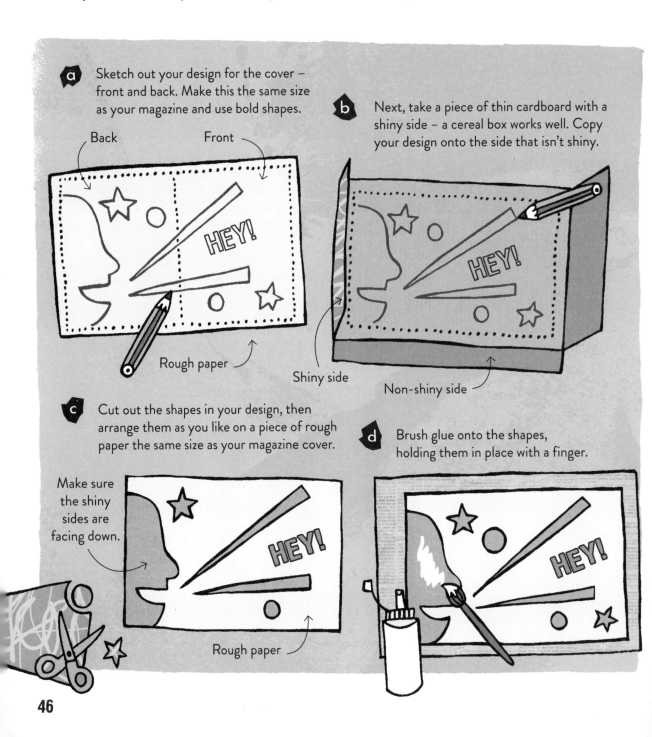

a. Sketch out your design for the cover – front and back. Make this the same size as your magazine and use bold shapes.

Back

Front

Rough paper

b. Next, take a piece of thin cardboard with a shiny side – a cereal box works well. Copy your design onto the side that isn't shiny.

Shiny side

Non-shiny side

c. Cut out the shapes in your design, then arrange them as you like on a piece of rough paper the same size as your magazine cover.

Make sure the shiny sides are facing down.

Rough paper

d. Brush glue onto the shapes, holding them in place with a finger.

HEY!

Take a piece of cardboard the same size as your magazine cover. Then, press it onto the shapes so they stick in place. This is your stamp.

Line up the edges of the cardboard and the paper.

 To use your stamp, brush paint onto the raised areas of shiny cardboard. Don't worry that you're painting on the back of your shapes – when you print they'll be facing the right way.

 Place the stamp paint-side down on top of the paper or cardboard you're using for your cover.

Rub it with the back of a spoon to print the paint onto the paper.

 Remove the stamp and leave the printed cover to dry. Repeat steps **f** and **g** to print more copies.

Make sure you print enough covers, plus a few spares, just in case.

Play with pages

Design surprising pages for your magazine to keep readers entertained.

Turn it round

Turn the magazine on its side to create a space that's a different shape. This might make room for a taller or bigger illustration.

ANIMALS OF THE SERENGETI

LIFE IN THE FAST LANE

PRETTY IN PINK

LIVING THE HIGH LIFE

Cut slices

Make one page into many, by cutting it into slices.

You could use the sliced page to reveal a secret identity or an astounding story, little by little.

It took us years to discover Mr. Cooper's big secret...

THINK TWICE BEFORE YOU SLICE

If you're going to slice up a page, make sure you plan both sides so you don't cut through anything by accident.

Trim a page

You could trim one page so it's shorter than the rest of your magazine. But you need to plan this carefully first.

Think about what parts of the page will be revealed when you turn the page.

You could turn the part you cut off into a bookmark to give away with your mag.

Read handmade magazines!

Punch a hole and add a ribbon.

Flip the corner

You could make a mini animation that moves when you flip the corner of a page.

Draw a picture in the corner of the first page. Keep it simple.

On the next page, draw the same picture, but with one change. The pictures must line up exactly for the animation to work.

To make a longer animation, draw a little picture on the corner of every page in your magazine. Flip quickly through all the corners with your thumb to watch it come to life.

Flip this corner up and down to see me in action.

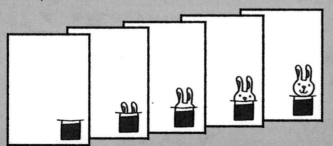

Decorating pages

Here are some ideas for easy ways to make the pages of your magazine look more exciting.

Fill blank space with dots or patterns...

...or scribbles for an alternative, "punk" look.

Add borders

TIP!

Don't go too close to the edge of the paper, or it might be cut off when you print or photocopy.

Jazz up the HEADINGS

Use words or letters cut out of old newspapers and glossy magazines.

Write by hand.

Try bubble writing.

If you're using a computer, you could use light writing on a dark background.

SLIME

Make your letter outlines wobbly and add some drips for slime writing.

BALLOONS

Turn bubble letters into balloons by adding a knot and string.

Use backgrounds

There are pages of textures and patterns at the back of this book you could use. A selection of these is available to download and print at the Usborne Quicklinks website.

You could make your own backgrounds by photocopying scraps of fabric or other objects.

Glitter can add extra bling.

You could add stickers.

Highlights

Use a highlighter to give your page some zing. This is great for picking out keywords, names or titles.

Use arrows to point your readers to what's important, or to show them what to read next.

USE A FLASH TO MAKE TEXT STAND OUT.

WATCH OUT!

Decoration can be distracting. Make sure it doesn't get in the way of reading.

If someone says something, put it in a speech bubble.

Pardon?

You heard me.

Putting it all together

You've got words and you've got pictures, so now it's time to transform them into a magazine. The next few pages are filled with handy hints on laying out pages, choosing a size and shape, printing, and getting your finished creations into the hands of readers.

HEADLINE

Shapes and sizes

Before you put your magazine together, you have to decide what shape and size (also known as format) it will be. The next six pages are full of format ideas to help you.

Booklets

Booklets are the most common format for magazines. They are made from two or more sheets of paper folded in half. Each sheet of paper becomes four pages in the booklet.

The sequence of pages can get a little confusing, so it's a good idea to number your pages.

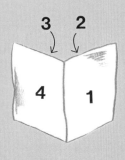

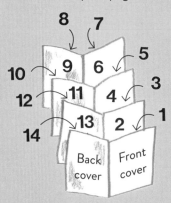

READ ME!

On page 56 you can find out how to secure the pages in place by binding them.

Fold-outs

Fold-outs are a more unusual format. They are made by folding just one long strip of paper. They can be as big or small, long or short as you like. There are tips for making a long strip on the next page.

Fold a strip of paper in a zig-zag.

Open out the pages to display its full glory...

I wonder what's on the other side?

This format is great for long pictures.

Turn to page 58 to see another format you can make from one long strip.

Giants

Use large sheets to make giant magazines. Don't worry if you only have regular-sized paper – you can tape or glue sheets together to make them larger.

Glue paper end to end to make long strips.

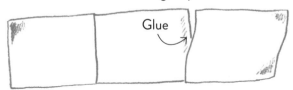

Glue

↑ Line up the top and bottom edges.

Or, to make large sheets for big booklets, stick the long edges together instead.

BABY ELEPHANTS!

ISSUE TWO

Minis

To make small magazines, cut up sheets of paper to make smaller pieces.

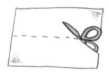

To make tiny strips, fold a sheet of paper in half lengthways, then open it out and cut along the fold.

Or to make pages for little booklets, fold and cut widthways.

Fold and cut again to make *really tiny*, pocket-sized magazines.

Tiny zine!

Mock it up

THIS IS EXTRA IMPORTANT!

Whatever format you go for, it's useful to make a mock-up. This is a blank, life-sized version of your magazine made from scrap paper.

Use your mock-up to:

- experiment with different ways of laying things out.
- make sure there are enough pages for everything to fit.
- check everything is in the right order and the correct way up.
- make sure different articles and pictures look good together.

Whether you're working big or small, if you are planning on making copies, make sure your magazine fits in the photocopier or printer.

Bold and stylish booklets

Here are ideas for different ways to bind your finished booklets so the pages stay in the right order. There are also some design tips.

Saddle stitch

Staple through the fold.

If your magazine is big or wide, you might need a long-armed stapler, like me.

Side binding

Staple through the side of your booklet.

Magazines bound like this won't open flat, though.

This technique works with any good stapler...

...and you can make booklets from separate sheets like this, too.

String binding

Cut a little notch at the top and bottom of the fold, through all the pages.

Wrap string around the fold, making sure it's tucked into the notches. Then, tie it in a tight knot.

Cut to here.

Cut to here.

Bow tie

Punch holes.

Thread a ribbon through the holes.

Tie a bow.

Flip it

Booklets don't have to open like a classic book – they could flip up.

Smart Casual
A fashion zine

Tips from Coco Chanel

"It is always better to be slightly underdressed."

Make rounded edges

NATURE JOURNAL

snip

snip

Use the edge of a coin as a stencil to draw around, then trim the corners.

Give it a profile

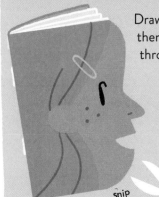

Draw a profile in pencil, then cut along the line through all the pages.

This one requires some planning, so you don't cut through anything important inside.

snip
snip

Put a jacket on it

You could make your magazine look extra special with a wrap-around jacket.

You'll need a piece of paper the same height as your folded pages and about three times the width of a single page.

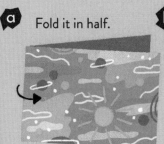

a Fold it in half.

b

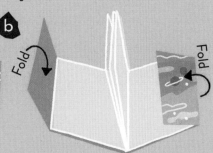

Fold

Fold

Tuck your zine into the middle crease, then fold the ends around the front and back covers.

One-sheet creations

Tall tales

You could make a tall zine. For this you'll need a long strip of paper. (If you don't have a sheet of paper long enough, tape or glue sheets together.)

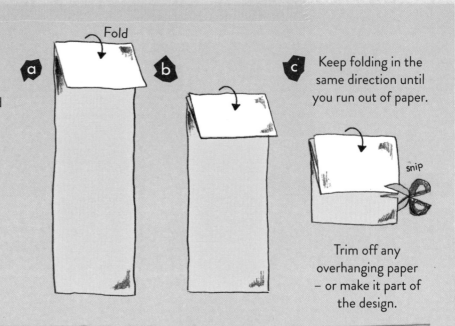

a Fold

b

c Keep folding in the same direction until you run out of paper.

snip

Trim off any overhanging paper – or make it part of the design.

This is the page sequence for a tall zine folded four times.

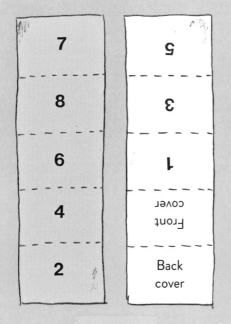

7	5
8	3
6	1
4	Front cover
2	Back cover

Unfold the strip to reveal two pages at a time.

"NNNRRGGH!!" THE LID WAS STUCK.

CASPAR PICKED UP THE JAR OF PICKLES.

You could combine text and pictures to tell a story.

Making a mock-up before you put together your final version will help you make sure everything is in the correct order.

Cabinet of curiosities

 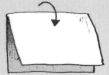

Fold a sheet of paper in half

 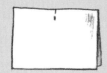

Pinch the middle of the folded edge – or mark it lightly with a pencil.

Fold in both sides to meet at the pinch mark.

Fill your cabinet with drawings or stick in pictures.

Add even more treasures to be revealed when the whole thing is unfolded.

Model boat

Shell

Thigh bone

Found key

One-sheet zine

This nifty zine, made from one sheet of paper, is perfect for small things, such as sketches of bugs or a collection of interesting words.

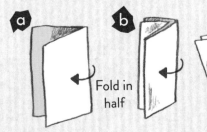

a **b** Fold in half **c** **d** Undo steps b and c, then cut.

Stop here

This is the sequence of pages.

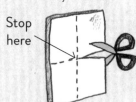

Front cover   Back cover

2	1	
3	4	5	6

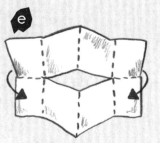

e Open the paper, then fold it long edge to long edge.

f Push

g Fold all the pages the same way to make a booklet.

The other side doesn't have to be blank.

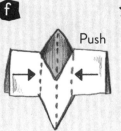 

What goes where?

Once you've chosen a format for your magazine, you'll need to gather everything together and decide what goes where.

Think about the order. You might not want to put a sad story after a page of jokes, or a comic starring a hen before a review of chicken sandwiches.

Alternating pictures and articles with lots of words helps vary the pace and keeps readers interested.

Make sure you start your magazine with a strong piece so readers are hooked from the start.

Once you're satisfied with the order, make a list, or note down on your mock-up what you want to include on each page.

Contents and intro — 1

Interview with Steve, school chef — 2

The perfect chicken sandwich — 3

Photographs of weird vegetables — 4

Readers' recipes — 5

Should I be a vegetarian? — 6

Space left over? Turn to page 29 for tips on last-minute space fillers.

Welcoming readers

You might want to use the first page or two of your magazine to set the scene for your readers.

> You could include a welcome note to introduce the theme of your magazine and pick out some of the highlights.

> If your magazine was a joint effort, you could include a list of contributors.

Welcome to WISE OWL, a magazine for all the family. This issue is all about summer vacation. There are top tips on what to do this summer, packing advice and a quiz to keep you entertained. Naomi has written about her camping trip and, as usual, Dad will be answering all your questions on our "What would Dad do?" page. I hope you enjoy it!

– Joe

Joe is editor-in-chief of WISE OWL. In his spare time, he goes to school and plays football.

Athena draws comics for WISE OWL. She wants to be an artist when she grows up.

> Remember to pack some books!

CONTENTS

Naomi is always planning adventures and wants to travel the world when she finishes school.

Dad has more than 10 years' experience of being a dad and almost 43 years' life experience.

> A list of contents will help readers navigate your magazine.

> You could include pictures, too.

Making layouts

A layout is the way text and pictures are set out on a page. There are computer programs for making layouts, but all you really need to create great page designs for your magazine are scissors and glue.

Make sure you have your pages in the correct order and right-side up. You could use your mock-up (see page 55) to check.

Give headings and titles room to stand out.

Pages in booklets won't always line up perfectly, so avoid running text across the join. You may need to leave extra space here for the binding.

Laying out text in narrow columns can make it easier to read.

Most printers and photocopiers don't print right to the edge, so don't put anything important in this area.

LONE WOLF

HOWL!

Is it clear which order you need to read the text? If not, you may need to number the text or add arrows.

Is a picture too big or too small? You can enlarge or shrink images using a photocopier.

Try out different arrangements. Don't glue anything down until you're satisfied with how the whole layout looks.

Master copy

Once you've put together all your layouts, you'll have a *master copy* of your magazine – the version all other copies are made from.

JOIN THE PACK

ISSUE 1

If you plan on making copies, don't bind it yet. Staples, strings and ribbons will get in the way.

Printing

If you want to share your magazine with others, you'll need to make copies. Here are some tips to help.

Photocopy

Zines are traditionally printed using a photocopier. If you've made your layouts by cutting and gluing, this is the easiest way to print.

Some photocopiers can even do the stapling for you.

You don't have to use white paper.

Use a printer

Printing with a standard printer is easy if you've been working on a computer, but if you haven't you'll need to scan your magazine pages first.

Printer ink can be expensive, so check with whoever owns the printer before you start.

IMPORTANT CHECKS

However you're planning on printing, make one copy first and check it carefully.

- ☐ Are the pages right-side up?
- ☐ Has anything important been cut off?
- ☐ Is all the text legible?
- ☐ Do the pictures show up?

Then you're ready to go ahead...

TEXT

Adjust the settings to make the printing lighter or darker if necessary.

Getting it out there

Once you've printed your handmade magazine, you need to decide how you're going to get it into the hands of readers and future fans.

Give it away

If friends and family like your magazine, they'll help spread the word.

Or alternatively...

Barter

Exchange magazines with other people and start building a collection.

Mail it

If you want to mail your magazine to people who live far away, make sure it is small and light enough for cheaper postage.

You could save on envelopes by designing your back cover with space for an address.

Fill in the address, tape up the sides, add a stamp and send it off.

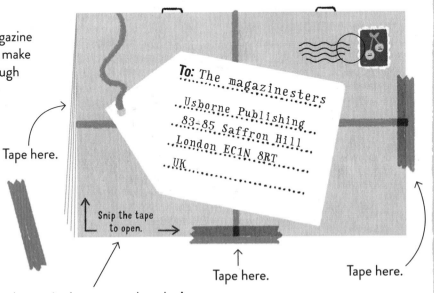

To: The magazinesters
Usborne Publishing
83-85 Saffron Hill
London EC1N 8RT
UK

Tape here.

Snip the tape to open.

Tape here.

Tape here.

Tell people to snip the tape, so they don't pull it off and damage the magazine.

Put it on display

Ask your school librarian if you can display your magazine for people to read. Alternatively, you could set up a stand at a school fair. You might even be allowed to sell your magazine.

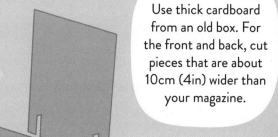

Use thick cardboard from an old box. For the front and back, cut pieces that are about 10cm (4in) wider than your magazine.

Make a stand to display your magazine prominently.

Cut slots about 3cm (1in) from the edge.

And cut slots in the two sides, where you want the back and front to fit into place.

Super Carrot saves the world...

...again!

Locally produced, fresh and extremely good value!

Slot the display together.

A sentence and some decoration will encourage readers to pick up a copy.

Marketing

Let your friends know your magazine will soon be out.

Coming soon!

Or ask to put an ad in someone else's handmade magazine.

Go digital

If you want to save paper, scan your magazine and email it to friends and family.

The next issue

It's never too soon to start thinking about the next issue of your magazine. In fact, it might be worth giving it some thought while you're working on the first issue. Here are some questions to think about and space to make notes...

Has the making of your first magazine gone smoothly?

Is there anything you'd do differently next time?

Which of your ideas has worked best?

Could you do something similar in the next issue?

Or maybe even a little better?

How often are you planning on making a magazine?

Weekly? Or monthly, maybe?

Get stuck in!

Over to you...

The following pages are yours to cut, rip, fold, photocopy, scrunch up, draw on, decorate and otherwise transform into pictures and pages for your homemade magazines. Cut or pull them out gently and get started.

If you want to use something from
these pages more than once, photocopy it.
A selection of these patterns and pictures
is also available to download from the
Usborne Quicklinks website.

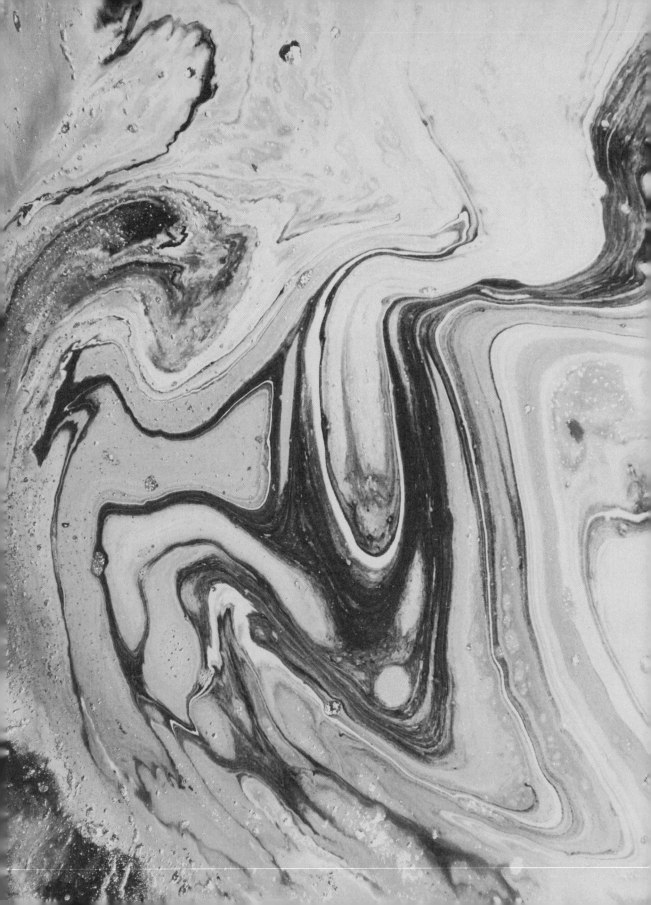

Build houses,
skyscrapers and walls.

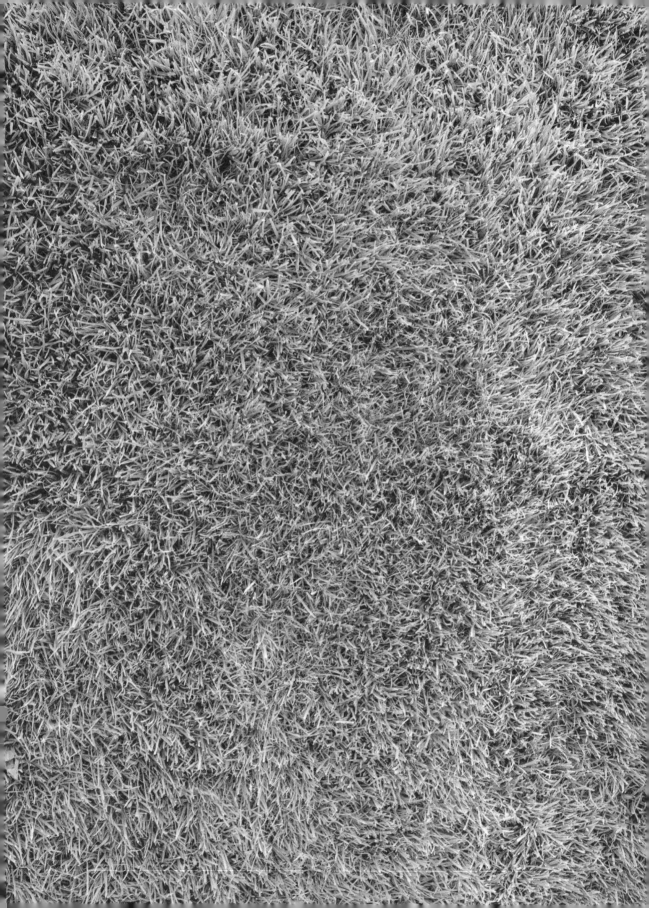

Show what you feel.

Use us as decoration!

Use these patterns to make borders and decorate pages.

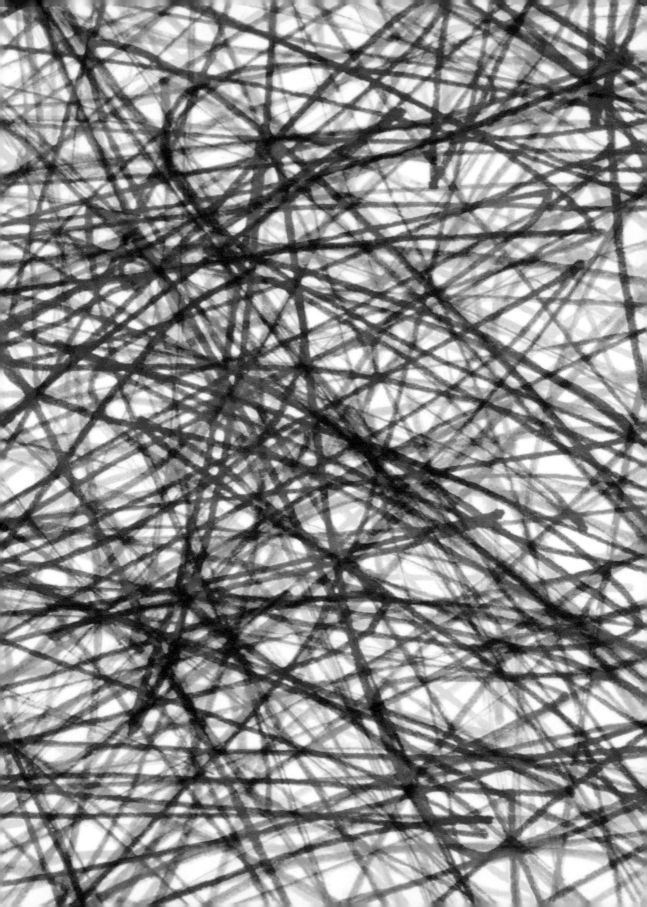

Notes and acknowledgements

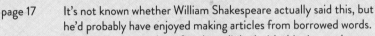

page 17   It's not known whether William Shakespeare actually said this, but he'd probably have enjoyed making articles from borrowed words.

page 20   Ernest Hemingway has often been linked with this six-word story, but he may not have actually written it.

page 21   The description of Miss Havisham comes from *Great Expectations* by Charles Dickens. "Make 'em..." is a quotation from Charles Reade, a novelist and a contemporary of Charles Dickens.

page 27   **The Athenian Mercury** was published twice weekly from March 1690 to June 1697.

page 34   Lewis Carroll included the poem "Jabberwocky" in his 1871 novel *Through the Looking-Glass, and What Alice Found There*.

page 57   "It is always..." is quoted in *Coco Chanel* by Isabella Alston and Kathryn Dixon, first published by TAJ Books International LLC in 2014.

Photographs on pages 11, 17, 21, 89 (Charles Dickens, William Shakespeare) © Depositphotos

Photographs on back cover (scissors, plug, multicolored squares paper) and pages 2, 3, 7, 9, 10, 15, 16, 24, 26, 30, 33, 36 (duck, hand, googly eyes, building, flower, pink grass, sheet music), 37 (bricks, frog's head, legs with red trainers, legs with walking boots, clown legs, skeleton, daffodils, camera, scissors), 38 (man), 39 (plug), 42, 45, 51 (cookie), 53, 54, 59, 62, 64, 66 (scissors, googly eyes, light bulb, sheet music), 67 (tabby cat, paws, sunglasses, dish), 69 (bricks), 70, 71, 72, 75, 76, 79, 85, 86, 89 (sunglasses, camera, duck, scissors, megaphone, alpaca, cactus, light bulb, cookie, flower, plug, bottom hand), 90, 93 © Dreamstime.com

Photographs on front cover, back cover (cat) and pages 8, 29, 36 (statue, newspaper), 37 (newspaper, cow legs, Queen Elizabeth I of England, bear), 46, 47, 60, 63, 66 (man), 67 (white cat), 69 (Queen Elizabeth I, cow), 89 (top hand, Queen Elizabeth I, cow, bear, white cat) © Thinkstock

Every effort has been made to trace and acknowledge ownership of copyright. If any rights have been omitted, the publishers offer their sincere apologies and will rectify this in subsequent editions following notification.

Additional illustration by Freya Harrison
Additional photography by Brian Voakes, Freya Harrison and Ray Moller
Additional cover illustration by Laurel Pettit
With thanks to models Francesca Tyler and Anthony Keates

The websites recommended at Usborne Quicklinks are regularly reviewed but Usborne Publishing is not responsible and does not accept liability for the availability or content of any website other than its own, or for any exposure to harmful, offensive or inaccurate material which may appear on the Web. Usborne Publishing will have no liability for any damage or loss caused by viruses that may be downloaded as a result of browsing the sites it recommends.

First published in 2019 by Usborne Publishing Ltd.,
Usborne House, 83-85 Saffron Hill, London EC1N 8RT, England.
www.usborne.com
Copyright © 2019 Usborne Publishing Ltd.

All rights reserved. No part of this publication may be reproduced, stored in a retrieval system or transmitted in any form or by any means, electronic, mechanical, photocopying, recording or otherwise, without the prior permission of the publisher. The name Usborne and the devices 🎈🎈 are Trade Marks of Usborne Publishing. AE. First published in America in 2019.